ADOPTING
BLOCKCHAIN
AND
CRYPTOCURRENCY

EMBRACING
A DIGITAL FUTURE

FRED LEE BRANDON III

ISBN: 978-1-7361796-1-1

Publisher: Lions Day Publishing
Edited by Nathan Paige and Dr. Tammy Francis
Foreword by Shadeed Eleazer
Cover and formatting by Waqar Nadeem

All inquiries should be sent to: fbrandon@fredbrandon.info

Contact:
https://fredbrandon.info
https://linkedin.com/in/fbrandon
https://linktr.ee/imfbrandon
Social Media: @imfbrandon

ABOUT THE AUTHOR

Originally from Cleveland, Ohio, he has spent the last two decades chasing his dreams while inspiring others to chase theirs. He enjoys using his creativity to solve problems.

As a technologist with over 20 years of IT experience, Fred has developed solutions and spoke at various venues across the globe. He's also a huge advocate for children and POC learning STEAM and financial programs. These include blockchain technology, Microsoft 365 & related applications, front end development, cryptocurrency, financial literacy, and children's literacy programs. He currently teaches blockchain globally with Althash University.

THE WHY

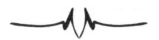

In this book, I want everyone to understand the importance of adopting blockchain technology and cryptocurrency as key components of how we interact now and in the future. Whether you're in the tech industry or just someone who wants to know more about cryptocurrency and future of banking, *Adopting Blockchain and Cryptocurrency* is the book for you. The future is now. The future is digital.

This book is primarily written for those who understand that if we are to progress, we must be innovative with our thought processes and technology. We cannot continue to use the same thinking and systems that created the mess that we are currently in and expect better results.

DEDICATION

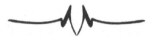

This book is dedicated to the two men who taught me work ethic and helped me learn the value of a dollar. Thank you, Fred Brandon Jr. and George Brandon Sr. To Mom, I appreciate all of your sacrifices and everything you taught me. I'd also like to thank my supporters, friends, mentors, and my family who has had my back from Day 1. A big shout out to those who helped me along this crypto and blockchain journey. A special thank you to PopFuzion TV for providing me a stage to "rant" about bitcoin even back in 2018. To everyone who has been in my corner, I appreciate your motivation and encouragement to always succeed.

CONTENTS

FOREWORD

There is a compound interest when it comes to decision making.

The choices we make today create a ripple effect that make our lives easier if we choose correctly according to our values, available information, and simply "what feels right".

The decisions that you make as an Investor hold a similar weight.

As a society, we've all read and heard about the employees within the legendary tech companies that have redefined how we live and work who held onto their company stock as the company grew into a tech giant. That decision changed their lives and the financial destiny of their lives and future generations of their offspring.

We often wait until we can see the grass is greener on the other side.

We often don't become early adopters because we heed the advice of experts and thought leaders, most of which are playing it safe.

What if there was an opportunity to be on the ground floor of a great opportunity? How would you respond?

In Adopting Blockchain and Cryptocurrency, Fred Brandon sets the scene for a new world built around decentralization using Blockchain technology. For the reader that is new to Blockchain, he outlines the essential terms and examples that you need to know to buckle up your seatbelt and dive into the solutions that are possible leveraging this emerging technology and philosophy for decentralized exchange.

Blockchain solves many problems that have emerged at the time of this release. Fortifying supply chains, essential government operations, creating a new, secure system of voting, and managing Intellectual Property are all within the realm of possibility.

This book is one part introductory guide, another part solutions manual, and a deep dive into the future with Fred Brandon as your expert navigator, helping you to see the world through a new and exciting lens.

We are embarking on a wild and exciting journey through creating new solutions leveraging Blockchain and Digital Assets. What makes Blockchain so compelling is at it's best, it encompasses exactly what technology was intended to do which is solve problems on a large scale and make life easier on a micro scale.

This guide contains several solutions that you'll want to refer back to 3 or 4 years from now, just to see how society has adopted them.

Fred Brandon sees the future and through Adopting Blockchain and Cryptocurrency and through reading these pages, you now have access to a time capsule that captured a rare moment in time with such clarity and accuracy that you don't see often.

Share this book with a friend or family who is curious about Blockchain and Cryptocurrency. Discuss this book with colleagues who are building cutting edge solutions. Give this book as a gift to decision-makers who are shaping the future of tomorrow's workforce.

The future belongs to those who lean into their decisions. Adopting Blockchain and Cryptocurrency is a bold look into what lies ahead. Enjoy, learn, and discuss the ideas that come from reading these pages.

Shadeed Eleazer - Philanthropist, Entrepreneur, Investor.

INTRODUCTION

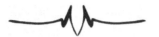

The dollar has fallen! Now, I know that may seem a little extreme, but the honest truth is, that it's not what it once was. How did we get here? If we are really being honest with ourselves, we all knew this day would eventually come.

Whether it is a politician, a celebrity, or any random promoter on Instagram, we are living in the era of social "influencers." We've been conditioned not to think for ourselves. We are constantly bombarded with images, slogans, and concepts that mold the way we think, eat, behave, and perceive our reality. In a system where we don't even govern ourselves or think for ourselves, why would we think that we should be in control of our own money? Ever since childhood, we have been told to put our money in the bank for "safe keeping." But is it really safe there? Yes, through FDIC we have some insurances in place, but overall is it in our best interest to keep our money there? (Pun intended)

Banks charge you to store your money. They charge you to take it out. They charge you if you don't have enough. Not only do they charge you to borrow their money (which is actually other people's money), they even charge you to borrow your own money. Tell me again, why are we stuck on this old banking philosophy?

What if you could be your own bank? What if you could lend it out and receive interest? What if you could send money to relatives across the world without exorbitant fees? What if there was no central entity governing your every financial move or taking their cut on all of your transactions?

This type of freedom is here. It exists with blockchain and cryptocurrency. Bitcoin, a popular cryptocurrency, is becoming an integral component in tackling many of the issues facing us with centralized banking. Before we attempt to understand cryptocurrency, let's first look at the foundation on which it's built.

I

BLOCKCHAIN

As we approach the next phase of computing, a new player, namely blockchain[1] technology, is revolutionizing the industry. Actually, the concept of blockchain has been around for over a decade, but its acceptance as a viable solution is becoming more widely accepted. So, what exactly is blockchain technology?

A blockchain is a distributed ledger[2] that uses cryptography[3] to ensure security, immutability, and accountability of transactions. Instead of storing information in a centralized location such as a database server, a blockchain decentralizes the information over multiple nodes or computers. Now, I know that sounds like a mouthful, so let's simplify that answer. Simply put, a blockchain consists of blocks of data chained together by the cryptographic hash[4] of the previous block[5]. By hashing the previous block, this ensures that the data has not been altered. Cryptography, a method of securing information mathematically by means of algorithms, provides the layer of security needed for blockchain to be successful.

A blockchain is decentralized and distributed and since it is not governed by one single entity, this adds an extra layer of security due to having no single point of failure. It acts as an immutable source of record, or a record that can't be changed once added to the blockchain. It can prevent fraud, provide transparency, enforce policies via smart contracts[6], streamline business processes, and allow you to securely collaborate, trustworthily, with known and unknown parties.

Blockchain – a type of distributed ledger consisting of blocks of data. Each block is then chained to the next block using a cryptographic hash referencing the previous block. This allows blockchains to be used like a ledger, which can be shared and accessed by anyone with the appropriate permissions.

Hash – A hash is the product of encrypting a string of any length to a random string of a fixed length. It can be used to easily verify that data has not been altered.

Another benefit of running a blockchain is the use of smart contracts. A smart contract is a program that runs on a blockchain that has been designed to automatically execute once the terms have been agreed upon by multiple parties. So, whether the parties are known or unknown, a smart contract can be utilized to be self-enforcing and self-executing. When creating smart contracts, it's best to cover every possible scenario to prevent loopholes.

Decentralized applications[7], or commonly referred to as "dapps," are programs that run on a distributed computing system like a blockchain and allows for user interaction. Decentralized applications are not governed by a single entity. They are highly customizable. So, whether you're playing a game, submitting medical information, or just conducting some type of business, dapps provide the means to allow interaction with the blockchain.

Smart Contracts – programs whose terms are recorded in computer languages instead of legal documents. They can be automatically executed by a distributed computing system, such as a blockchain like Ethereum. These contracts are designed to be tamper-proof and settle contract breaches automatically.

DApps – Decentralized applications, or dApps, are programs that allow a user to interact directly with a blockchain and are not governed by a single entity.

Defining what a blockchain is, is only part of the equation. What are its capabilities? Is it just the newest, shiniest toy? Does it have real-world usage? The real question is, does your infrastructure really need a blockchain? Let's get a little more in-depth by discussing why you should consider blockchain, along with ways it can be used in your industry.

WHY CONSIDER BLOCKCHAIN?

You may be wondering if your business really needs to pursue a blockchain solution. The easy answer is, "it depends." Just like with any tech solution, a blockchain is just one tool that can facilitate a need. It is necessary to take an accurate assessment of your environment to determine if a blockchain is required. Unfortunately, this may not always happen. Many businesses are quick to jump onboard with the latest and greatest without doing their due diligence. How many times has an exec made a decision based on what a competitor was doing? More than they'll ever admit. Trying to shoehorn any solution when it's not right for your environment is an easy setup for failure.

Truth be told, many systems in the business world are antiquated and inefficient. "If it isn't broken, why fix it?" Oftentimes, complacency has become our greatest enemy when it comes to solving our business' pain points. Waiting until it is broken, will undoubtedly be more expensive in the long-run. The key is to remain proactive when it comes to your systems and processes. COVID-19 has forced many companies to not only rethink their strategies, but take an honest inventory of their current systems and make the necessary adjustments. Many companies are probably already using some form of cloud solution or maintaining their environment locally in a datacenter. Platforms such as SharePoint, Salesforce,

Microsoft 365, Dynamics, and SAP are the go-to when it comes to business solutions and collaboration.

What happens when these platforms aren't enough?

As a solution architect, it is important to weigh all the options before implementing a strategy. Will it be a blockchain? A cloud solution? Maybe a hybrid solution? Factors like time, money, and level of effort will always play a major role in this decision-making process.

You can start by asking yourself these questions?

- Does this need to be a collaborative effort?

- If so, are all the actors within the organization?

- Will all the contributors be known or unknown?

- Will this solution allow for scale?

- Can the assets be digitized?

- Is encryption necessary?

- Will the history of state need to be recorded?

- Is it cost-effective?

- What's the ROI?

So, when determining whether you should use a blockchain or cloud solution, tools like the CAUSE matrix can help justify which solution is the best fit.

- C – Collaborative workflow

- A – Assets digitized

- U – Unknown or known Contributors

- S – Storage of state necessary

- E – Encryption crucial

Collaborative Workflow	Assets Digitized?	Unknown Contributors?	Storage of State?	Encryption Crucial?	Blockchain Required?	Type of Blockchain
Yes	Yes	Yes	Yes	Yes	Yes	Public
Yes	Yes	No	Yes	Yes	Yes	Private
Yes	Yes	Both	Yes	Yes	Yes	Hybrid
No	Yes	Yes	No	Yes	No	Cloud
Yes	No	Yes	Yes	No	No	Cloud

FIGURE 1: CAUSE MATRIX VIA UNLOCKING BLOCKCHAIN ON AZURE, KARKERAA, 2020.

As we can see from this matrix, depending on what's actually needed, we can determine if we need a cloud, public, private, or hybrid blockchain solution. Public blockchains can be compared to the Internet, while private blockchains are more like a company's private intranet. Bitcoin is an example of a public blockchain.

When architecting your solution, remember it's not all or nothing. You don't have to decide cloud or blockchain. You can still have both. Even with your current web apps, mobile apps, and even IoT devices, you're able to create custom solutions that not only interact with off-chain applications such as Azure SQL database, Azure Blob storage, and the Power Platform, but these can also be incorporated into your blockchain solution. You just need to decide when it's right to use each one.

Not every company will need a fully architected end-to-end blockchain solution. Fortunately, companies like Microsoft Azure, Amazon Web Services, and Althash have blockchain-as-a-service, or BaaS, strategies that can make it easier to integrate blockchain into a company's current infrastructure.

USE CASES

Just like any technology, blockchain itself is a tool and should be viewed as such. Will it fix every problem? No. Does it have many use cases? Absolutely. We are seeing more and more companies implement blockchain technology as a viable solution to their infrastructure. Companies like Starbucks, Liberty Mutual Insurance, Sony Music, and others have already incorporated blockchain into their infrastructure to address issues in their supply chain or policy management.

The use case for blockchain technology has been seen across various industries including healthcare, supply chain, government, and more. Imagine the transparency of being able to track a process from end to end to ensure quality of a product. For instance, when tracking produce from the farm to your grocery store, the legal documents when closing on a property, or even creating a digital ID for voting, you can have that reassurance that the food is safe for consumption or the legal information has not been modified by implementing blockchain into your solution.

Let's look at a few real-world instances where blockchain is already being used.

Industry	Use Case
Healthcare	An accessible record of a patient's medical history on the blockchain. This can be used to understand previous conditions, allergies, and medications to provide better diagnoses and solutions.
Supply Chain	Whether it's food, wine, or clothing, a blockchain can track products within the chain, identify issues, and verify authenticity of items.
Intellectual Property	If you're creating digital artwork, patents, or filing trademarks, a blockchain can verify ownership of intellectual property.
Voting	Voting suppression and fraud continues to be a concern during every election. Employing a blockchain solution for voting can create a verifiable system with timestamps and digitally link to a registered voter.
Energy	Solar panels, smart meters, along with blockchain technology can provide a clear picture of energy consumption and production to increase efficiency and reduce costs of resources.

As we see, regardless whether it's government, financial, retail, or healthcare, there are many opportunities to incorporate blockchain technology into your company's initiative. In recent years, the financial sector has seen a huge upswing of adoption in blockchain with the introduction of cryptocurrency[8]. Let's see how blockchain, along with cryptocurrency are becoming global phenomena.

II

CRYPTOCURRENCY

QUOTE

"It's just money. It's made up. Pieces of paper with pictures on it so that we don't have to kill each other just to get something to eat."
– *John Tuld, Margin Call*

"Give a man a gun and he can rob a bank, but give a man a bank and he can rob the world."
– *Tyrell Wellick, Mr. Robot*

What is money? If you ask the average person, they'll probably tell you it's the way you pay for stuff. But what is it actually? If you really think about it, the same paper and ink are being used, but a computer is programmed to print the number 1, 5, 10, etc. In actuality, we are only honoring that ink of those numbers at the respective values. Really? The actual paper is worthless, but we have agreed to assign a corresponding value to each denomination. With that being said, we can understand currency as an asset that has an attributed value.

For stability, some currencies are backed by some sort of resource like gold or oil to maintain that value. What about the U.S. Dollar? Is it backed by something? Well, the U.S. Dollar hasn't been backed by gold since 1971. Unless there's someone in the basement of the Treasury spinning straw into gold, a country can just print more money any time they want. Where is the real value?

This is the only system many of us have ever known. You may be asking, "if it's not broke, why should we fix it?" Truth is, it is broken and has always been. Some of us have just found ways to make the best of a bad situation. Others have always been behind the 8-ball. Banks have always been crooked and only truly benefits those who can afford it and understand how it works. The majority of society will probably fall victim to predatory loans whether it's for school, a home, or a vehicle.

Even with knowledge of this, central banks are used as a "trusted entity" between the consumer and the merchant. But at what cost? Shouldn't you be able to make transactions with whomever without a middleman charging fees to do so? I would hope so.

Enter cryptocurrency.

What exactly is cryptocurrency? Well, the first part of the word "crypto" is short for cryptography. Cryptography is a method of securing information with code between the sender and the recipient. So, cryptocurrency is a digital asset that stores a particular value and uses cryptography as the means to secure it between two parties.

Cryptocurrency, or crypto for short, is a form of digital currency based on mathematics, where cryptography and digital signatures are used to regulate the generation of units of currency and verify the transfer of funds.

In recent years, the topic of crypto is becoming a steady buzzword in many conversations as a new form of currency. Bitcoin, in particular, is the forerunner of all cryptocurrency conversations. Understanding bitcoin, is just as important as understanding why it was necessary.

Bitcoin is not as young as many may think; it was introduced to the world in 2009 by the unknown entity, Satoshi Nakamoto. The philosophy of bitcoin is to be a peer-to-peer[9] network that allows for transactions to be made to each other without the need of a financial institution acting as a mediator. It also solves the double-spend[10] problem with using a peer-to-peer (P2P) network. Double-spending is the act of trying to spend the same asset more than once before it has been properly recorded or checked. I encourage everyone to read the bitcoin whitepaper on bitcoin.org/bitcoin.pdf. It's only about 9 pages long, but it lays out a solid foundation of understanding this peer-to-peer system of managing transactions.

Peer-to-peer – A network that operates without the need for a central server or point of control. In a peer-to peer (P2P) network, people are able to interact without a middleman.

Double-spending – The process of attempting to spend coins that have already been spent in another transaction.

Despite being around for over a decade, bitcoin has had a slow start with mainstream adoption. In 2017, we began to see a little more traction as the price began to rise. Even at the time of this writing, it has yet to be fully accepted as a form of currency in many places in the world.

If it solves problems, why has it taken so long for a wider acceptance?

One of the main reasons why society has been slow to accept bitcoin is due a lack of understanding the technology on which it relies. Blockchain technology is the foundation on which bitcoin and other cryptocurrencies are supported. A blockchain allows you to decentralize information, processes, and even currencies while ensuring accountability, security, and immutability on a distributed ledger. This technology may seem foreign to many, but society has been groomed for it for many years.

Another reason is some people can't get past the concept of touching physical money. If it's not tangible, they don't think of it as real. But as we mentioned before, money is really just an assigned value and therefore it doesn't need to be tangible.

Through the years, we have been accustomed to having some type of physical "money," whether paper or a coin. But when you really think about it, credit cards are actually cashless and they've been around for decades. By using a credit or debit card, you are simply transferring the amount from your account (ledger) to the merchant's account or ledger.

Remember checks? Yes, they worked the same way as digital money does. Each check had a routing number, an account number, an amount, and a physical signature.

With digital currency, transactions will be made between ledgers via wallet addresses[11].

Now, with the introduction of peer-to-peer (P2P) systems like PayPal, Cash App, Venmo, and others, you have an entire world making daily transactions without ever touching physical "money."

GETTING STARTED

When we look into cryptocurrencies, it may be a little confusing at first. Including bitcoin, there are currently over 5,000 cryptocurrencies. You may have heard the term altcoin[12] before. To simplify, altcoins are basically all coins besides bitcoin. This can be a little overwhelming at first glance. Let's break down different types of digital currency terminology.

Term	Definition	Example
Coin	An asset native to its own blockchain.	Bitcoin, Ether, Litecoin
Token	Tokens are created on existing blockchains.	ERC20, NEP5, HRC20
Utility	Used to provide access to a product or service.	Golem, Civic, OmiseGo
Privacy	Transactions are kept private between sender & recipient	ZCash, Monero, Dash

Payment	Used to pay for goods and services	Bitcoin, Litecoin, Bitcoin Cash
Stablecoin	Crypto built to retain a stable value, usually backed with fiat[13].	USD Coin, Tether, Dai
Security	Token used in ownership stake of a company.	Blockchain Capital, Sia, Slice
CBDC	The central bank's fiat in digital currency.	Bank of Ghana, Banco Central do Brasil, Eastern Caribbean Central Bank

Fiat – A government issued currency that isn't backed by a commodity such as gold and holds no intrinsic value.

CBDCs

Cryptocurrencies can operate independently of a central bank. In fact, the whole purpose of decentralization[14] and crypto was to remove the need of a central governing entity. This has not prevented central banks with coming up with their own digital currencies in an effort to not be left behind in this digital revolution. Central bank digital currencies, or CBDCs, allows them to manage their fiat as a digital currency. Now, while I agree with the advent of CBDCs for bringing more adoption to cryptocurrency, I also feel like this is the same dog with a different dress. It introduces the masses to digital currencies, but it does not address the need for decentralization.

ACQUISITION AND MANAGEMENT

Now that we know the differences between the various types of crypto, you may decide to acquire some. If you do, there are a few things that you should know. When acquiring crypto, you will more likely be on some sort of an exchange to buy, sell, or trade.

Exchanges, like Coinbase and Binance, are the main way of acquiring cryptocurrencies. Not all exchanges are created equal, so be sure to do your own research (DYOR[15]) when registering with an exchange. Coins, transaction fees, and policies will vary on each platform, so be sure to choose wisely. Many exchanges will require that you adhere to their AML[16] (Anti-Money Laundering) and KYC[17] (Know Your Customer) policies in order to conduct trades on their platform. You may be required to submit a government-issued ID or passport in order to satisfy this requirement.

Once you have secured some crypto, it is best practice to have a safe place to store it. I would suggest storing it in a wallet[18], instead of keeping it in the exchange wallet. Over the years, there have been numerous hacks to the exchanges. A wallet allows you to securely store your cryptocurrency. There are several types of wallets, but basically you have hot wallets and cold wallets. Hot wallets are connected to the Internet and are typically on your phone or computer. Cold wallets are not connected to the Internet, making them considerably the best way to store your crypto. Paper wallets are merely printed keys or QR codes, but is no longer considered a safe method of securing your crypto.

Hosted wallets are also a way to store crypto, but they're not recommended. Some apps like Robinhood may allow you to buy or sell bitcoin, but remember "not your keys, not your crypto." Some apps will not allow you to purchase or send your crypto. So, your best bet is to grab a secure wallet, preferably offline to store your keys.

It's better to be safe than sorry, so make sure to understand which wallet is best for you. A good resource for choosing a wallet is https://bitcoin.org/en/choose-your-wallet.

Wallet – A solution or device that stores a user's private and public keys.

Your public and private keys are your claim to the crypto that you own. The public key[19] can be likened to your email address, and the private key[20] can be likened to your password. In the same way you would never disclose your password to your email account, you should never disclose your private key. Otherwise, you risk losing access to your crypto.

TRANSACTIONS

In this day and age, we are conducting more business transactions on a global level. Whether it's B2B (business-to-business), C2C (customer-to-customer), or just sending money to family, our options to conduct transactions are often limited and come with high fees. Services like Western Union and MoneyGram are known to have cash limits, high fees, and in some cases a processing wait time. Not to mention, if you're sending funds to an underbanked area, the delay could be even longer.

Crypto solves this problem by being borderless. It also provides the ability to send money internationally and nearly instantaneously without the exorbitant fees. Just like popular apps PayPal and Cash App, sending and receiving crypto has been simplified by directing funds to a wallet address.

Address – a digital currency address is used to receive and send transactions from and to other users on the network, similarly to an email address. An address is a string of alphanumeric characters, but can also be represented as a scannable QR code.

ADOPTION

Adoption as a society is the key. The need for both blockchain and cryptocurrencies will continue to make its presence felt. As previously mentioned, governments, financial institutions, hospitals, and other industries are already incorporating blockchain technology into their plans for the future. There is no time like the present to start embracing blockchain as a new skill or understanding the importance of investing or making transactions with cryptocurrencies. The sooner we realize the need for adoption, the easier it will be to adjust to the future of how we conduct business.

GLOSSARY & KEY TERMS

Address – a digital currency address is used to receive and send transactions from and to other users on the network, similar to an email address. An address is a string of alphanumeric characters, but can also be represented as a scannable QR code.

Altcoin – Any coin other than bitcoin

AML – Anti-Money Laundering

Block – A data structure containing aggregated transactions data. Blocks are cryptographically linked together to form the larger data structure called a blockchain. The first block in any given blockchain is called the genesis block.

Blockchain – A blockchain is a distributed ledger that uses cryptography to ensure security, immutability, and accountability of transactions. Instead of storing information in a centralized location such as a database server, a blockchain decentralizes the information over multiple nodes or computers.

Cryptocurrency – A form of digital currency based on mathematics, where cryptography and digital signatures are used to regulate the generation of units of currency and verify the transfer of funds. Cryptocurrencies operate independently of a central bank.

Cryptography – A method of securing information mathematically by means of algorithms between two parties.

DApps – DApps, or decentralized applications, are programs that allow a user to interact directly with a blockchain.

Distributed Ledger – a distributed ledger is a type of data structure that is spread across multiple sites, countries, or institutions. Distributed ledger data can be either permissioned or unpermissioned to control who can read and write to the ledger.

Decentralization – the process by which the activities of an organization are distributed away from a central authoritative location or group.

Double-spend – The process of attempting to spend coins that have already been spent in another transaction.

DYOR – Do your own research

Fiat – A government issued currency that isn't backed by a commodity such as gold.

FOMO – Fear of missing out

FUD – Fear, uncertainty, and doubt

Hash – A hash is the product of encrypting a string of any length to a random string of a fixed length. It can be used to easily verify that data has not been altered because if any part of the input data has changed and the hash algorithm is run again, the hash will change.

HODL – Holding on for dear life or simply holding an asset

KYC – Know Your Customer

Miner – A person who uses mining hardware/software that is designed to spend computational resources toward confirming transactions into a block and verifying the network.

Mining – The process by which transactions are verified and added to a proof of work blockchain. This process of solving cryptographic problems using high-powered, specialized computing hardware also triggers the generation of cryptocurrencies.

Peer-to-peer – A network that operates without the need for a central server or point of control. In a peer-to peer (P2P) network, people are able to interact without a middleman.

Permissioned Ledger – A permissioned ledger only allows a select number of parties to read or write data to the shared ledger.

Private Key – a cryptographic key that allows you to authorize and sign digital transactions from a given address. Private keys can be thought of as passwords. Private keys must never be revealed to anyone, as they allow you to spend digital currencies using a cryptographic signature.

Proof of Stake – An alternative to a proof of work system that validates transactions or ledger updates based on the number of digital tokens you currently possess or stake.

Proof of Work – a system that ties mining capability to computational power. Blocks must be hashed with an additional parameter, which requires many tries to compute a valid hash. A successfully hashed block is considered proof of computational work.

Public key – a cryptographic key that encrypts code and can only be decrypted by its corresponding private key. A public key can be openly shared.

Smart Contracts – contracts whose terms are recorded in computer languages instead of legal documents. They can be automatically executed by a distributed computing system, such as a blockchain like Ethereum. These contracts are designed to be tamper-proof and settle contract breaches automatically.

Solution Architect – a person responsible for the design of one or more applications or services that integrates information and computer systems to address the needs of an organization.

Unpermissioned Ledger – unpermissioned ledgers like Bitcoin blockchain have no single owner. The goal of an unpermissioned ledger is to allow anyone to contribute data to the ledger and for everyone in possession of the ledger to maintain an identical copy. Participants maintain the integrity of the ledger by reaching a consensus about its state.

Use Case – a specific situation in which a product or service could potentially be used.

Wallet – A solution that stores a user's private and public keys.

CPSIA information can be obtained
at www.ICGtesting.com
Printed in the USA
BVHW072220120421
604726BV00004B/787